Bishops in Communion

Collegiality in the Service of the *Koinonia* of the Church

AN OCCASIONAL PAPER OF THE
HOUSE OF BISHOPS OF
THE CHURCH OF ENGLAND

CHURCH HOUSE
PUBLISHING

Church House Publishing
Church House
Great Smith Street
London SW1P 3NZ

ISBN: 0 7151 5759 0

Published 2000 for the Council for Christian Unity by Church House Publishing

This report has been approved by the House of Bishops.

Acknowledgement

The Scripture quotations contained herein are from The New Revised Standard Version of the Bible, Anglicized Edition, copyright © 1989, 1995 by the Division of Christian Education of the National Council of the Churches of Christ in the United States of America, and are used by permission. All rights reserved.

Printed in England by Halstan & Co. Ltd

Contents

Foreword

During the past ten years, the House of Bishops of the Church of England has been aware of the need to strengthen the theological foundations of its work. Following debate in the General Synod on the report *Episcopal Ministry*, the House requested the Faith and Order Advisory Group of the Council for Christian Unity to work on the theology and practice of episcopal collegiality. What does it mean for bishops to work together as one body? How does this help to ensure that the Church is maintained in that unity in the truth for which Christ prayed? What theological principles undergird episcopal collegiality? How does this reflect and enhance the ministry and mission of the whole priestly body of the Church? *Bishops in Communion* is the product of several years' work by the Faith and Order Advisory Group in consultation with the House of Bishops. We are grateful to the Chairman (the Bishop of Gibraltar in Europe), members and staff of the Faith and Order Advisory Group for this substantial and helpful report. We commend it for study and reflection by bishops, members of the General Synod and all with a concern for leadership in the Church of Christ.

On behalf of the House of Bishops of the Church of England

✠ GEORGE CANTUAR   ✠ DAVID EBOR
Archbishop of Canterbury   Archbishop of York

September 1999

Introduction

In January 1991 the General Synod debated *Episcopal Ministry: The Report of the Archbishops' Group on the Episcopate* (The Cameron Report). A covering paper (GS 955) by the Standing Committee of the General Synod said:

> The Standing Committee intends that, following the Synod debate, the report should be referred formally to the House of Bishops and to the Dioceses' Commission for their views. Once these are available, the Standing Committee will itself consider the report further in the light of the Synod debate, before reporting back to the Synod with specific recommendations.

Following the Synod debate, the House of Bishops' Theological Group identified three issues needing further consideration: the collegiality of bishops; apostolicity and succession; and suffragan bishops. The House invited the Faith and Order Advisory Group (FOAG) to prepare papers on apostolicity and succession, and collegiality. The work of FOAG on apostolicity and succession was published as an Occasional Paper of the House of Bishops in May 1994. This present paper is a response to the request for work on collegiality.

The reasons for developing a common understanding of collegiality include the following:

1.   The House of Bishops in recent years has played an increasingly significant role in forming and articulating the mind of the Church of England on matters of faith, order and moral teaching. This is seen in the lead the bishops gave in the report *The Nature of Christian Belief*, the work of the House of Bishops on the ordination of women to the priesthood, the House's guidance in the document *Issues in Human Sexuality* and, most recently, *Eucharistic Presidency*.

2.   The leadership of the bishops, gathered together at the Lambeth Conference in 1978 and 1988, was important in guiding the Anglican Communion in the matter of the ordination of women to the presbyterate and the episcopate, as well as in the formation of an Anglican Communion response to the multilateral and bilateral

ecumenical reports, *Baptism, Eucharist and Ministry* and *The Final Report* of ARCIC.

3. Collegiality has now become a subject treated in many ecumenical dialogues, as those dialogues have sought to understand more about the gifts of communion that maintain Christians in a united life.

Since this work was begun in 1994, discussions of the Turnbull Report, *Working as One Body*, and the Bridge Report, *Synodical Government in the Church of England*, have shown that an understanding of collegiality is vital for any restructuring of leadership in the Church of England today. It is hoped that this paper will help the Church of England as it seeks to develop structures and processes of discernment, decision-making and reception which will serve the faithful and effective proclamation of the gospel at the beginning of the next millennium.

Discussions about the nature and function of bonds of communion within the Church of England and the Anglican Communion are part of a much wider contemporary debate. Almost every church, both in its internal life and in its relations with other churches, faces questions of identity, coherence and the structures that are able to hold Christians in committed fellowship, discerning the faith together and being empowered for mission.

In the multilateral discussions in the World Council of Churches the subject of conciliarity and conciliar fellowship has been a concern for many years. The Faith and Order Commission has recently published a study of *episkope* in the service of the *koinonia* of the Church, following on requests made in the responses of the churches to *Baptism, Eucharist and Ministry*. The Commission is continuing this work in the context of its study on the nature and purpose of the Church. Many bilateral dialogues have also addressed the question of the bonds of visible unity, with some remarkable convergences emerging. The recent work of the Anglican – Roman Catholic International Commission on the gift of authority is contributing to this exploration. Moreover, the discussion of collegiality and primacy has recently been given a new impetus by Pope John Paul II's invitation to engage with him in an exploration of the ministry of primacy in the service of unity. This gives added relevance to the subject of this report. At the invitation of the Archbishop of Canterbury, FOAG prepared a draft response to *Ut Unum Sint* for the House of Bishops of the Church of England which the bishops developed further and published in December 1997 under the title *May They All Be One*.

When FOAG began its work on collegiality, it was aware that although certain ecumenical documents, as well as the work of the Inter-Anglican Theological and Doctrinal Commission, touch on collegiality, there is no fully developed ecumenical or Anglican theology of collegiality. Though successive Lambeth Conferences have reflected on their own collegial role and authority, the subject is a relatively new one in Anglican ecclesiology. Neither is there in practice a full expression of the ministry of collegiality while churches remain separated. Our task was, therefore, in a large measure one of reflecting theologically on experience. When we reflected upon the developing collegial structures of the Church of England and of the Anglican Communion, it was possible to discern something of the significance of collegiality for the life of the Church and its potential for making more effective the Church's witness in the world. The collegiality of bishops serves both to strengthen the internal life of the Church and to make more effective its missionary vocation. Further, as we gained a better understanding of the significance of collegiality in the Church of England and the Anglican Communion, we began also to understand something of the place that collegiality might play in serving the visible unity of the one, holy, catholic and apostolic Church.

In exploring the issue of collegiality FOAG became convinced that it was best set within an understanding of the Church as a communion or fellowship (*koinonia*) in which every member has a part to play. Collegiality belongs within the interdependent life of the whole people of God and relates to the various means by which that life is ordered and held together. Collegiality cannot be understood apart from the life of the whole Church. Questions of collegiality are closely related to questions of conciliarity (synodality) and primacy. Moreover, episcopal collegiality is integrally related to the maintenance of the unity, holiness, catholicity and apostolicity of the Church.

In Chapter 1 we reaffirm what we believe is fundamental to an understanding of the nature of the Church, namely the Church as *koinonia*, the fellowship of those reconciled with God through Jesus Christ and with one another in the life and love of God. In Chapter 2 we explore the God-given gifts which sustain Christians within the communion of the Church. Chapter 3 considers collegiality and its relation to conciliarity and primacy in the service of the communion of the Church. Chapter 4 reflects on the use of power and authority in maintaining communion. Finally, in Chapter 5 the report looks at collegiality today as it serves the unity of the Church of England, the Anglican Communion and emerging ecumenical structures. This last chapter raises a number of issues for further study about the development of collegiality within the Church of England, the Anglican Communion and the ecumenical movement.

1

The Church as *Koinonia*

Why *koinonia*?

In recent years *koinonia* has become an increasingly important theme in the ecumenical movement and in the Anglican Communion, and has revitalized our understanding of the nature of the Church and of its visible unity. The reasons for this are interesting and complex. Ecumenical dialogues and reflection on them have led the churches to think more deeply about the unity to which Christians are called.

The unity of the Church is not a thing in itself, but is inseparable from what we believe about the nature of God, the universe as the creation of God and God's ultimate purposes for it. This in turn leads to questions about the relationship between the Church and the rest of creation, and to an exploration of the theme of the kingdom of God. What is the nature of the fellowship, sharing or communion which unites, presently and potentially, all that God has made? Furthermore, the Christian doctrine of creation means that these matters cannot properly be understood apart from what we know of God's own being and activity.

In speaking about *koinonia*, therefore, we are not merely talking about the Church. We are trying to understand something of what the Church means in God's purposes and in relation to God's own being.

God is revealed as Father, Son and Holy Spirit, and we trace the activity and even something of the nature of this Triune God as we contemplate the created universe and confess God to be creator, saviour and sanctifier. In all these ways we discover God to be the maker and ruler of all things, so that the underlying structure of reality is already one of communion, albeit marred and frustrated. Creation is open to, indeed is oriented towards, a participation in God's own communion of mutual love. It follows that if the Church is in any way an instrument for proclaiming and revealing God's rule, *koinonia* will also be a central way of understanding the Church itself.

1

The communion of the Holy Trinity

In the early, formative, centuries of the Christian era, the Church came to understand that the relationship between Jesus Christ and his heavenly Father, which is signified in the gospel by the Spirit descending on Jesus at his baptism, was not simply something God willed for a particular time and in a particular set of circumstances, but is rather part of God's eternal being and purpose. Rather than speaking about a remote and impersonal deity, Christianity spoke from the outset about a God who is a communion (*koinonia*) of 'persons'.

The act of creation is entirely appropriate for such a God, whose nature is already personal and relational, and whose loving communion is both revealed and reflected in an outward movement of unstinting generosity. This movement is described as the mission of the Son and of the Holy Spirit and is seen not only in creation, but also in God's unceasing outreach in love to reconcile and restore the scattered fragments of what God has made in and for love. In the Old Testament we read of God's attempts to restore the covenant with his chosen people. In the New Testament we read both about God's ultimate purpose to reconcile all things with Jesus Christ as head, and also about the cost of that reconciliation in the cross. It follows that nothing is so small as to be beneath God's notice, nor so estranged as to be beyond God's care. This helps us understand the particular concern God shows through the prophets and above all through Jesus Christ for the 'lost, the last and the least'. In short, the mission of God is oriented in creation and restoration towards establishing or re-establishing God's rule (kingdom) over all things, and bringing them into a relationship of communion with himself and one another.

Koinonia and the kingdom of God

The communion which is proper to God's own nature is a characteristic both of the divine life and, potentially and eschatologically, of the universe as God's creation. In Christ God was reconciling the world to his own communion of love.

This perspective points to the necessity and significance of difference or diversity within the created order. Without difference there can be no relationship; but without relationship difference degenerates into discord and conflict. Discord is not a possibility between the persons of the Holy Trinity, whose communion arises from the Father as the sole cause and origin. In the created world likewise, it is the common origin of all things which gives unity, but for its preservation this unity requires a constant dependence on God: Father, Son and Holy Spirit. Whatever the cause or causes of the fallen state of the world, the consequences of alienation from God certainly include alienation and conflict between the different components of the universe. It becomes difficult to distinguish between those differences which are part of the God-given richness of creation and those which are themselves signs of failure and sin. It is however clear that restoration to God means restoration to communion and that this in turn implies the re-establishment of God's kingly reign over a renewed communion.

Kingdom, world, Church

It has become commonplace to assert the importance of the logical sequence 'kingdom – world – Church'. This is often a necessary corrective to the wrong kind of preoccupation with ecclesiastical life and structures. On the other hand it is important not to misunderstand the relationship between the three. The kingdom is the goal of creation, the end for which the world was created, and of which the Church is a sign, instrument and foretaste. As such the Church is both a sign of the kingdom and a terrestrial reality. As a sign and foretaste of the kingdom, the Church already enjoys the communion of heaven; as an instrument of God's mission, the Church remains in solidarity with fragmented earthly 'community', and through the failures of its members the Church, which is to be presented without spot or wrinkle, continues to be stained by human sin. Idealistic tendencies in ecclesiology must always be resisted, as too must those which treat the Church as merely a sociological and historical phenomenon. Through its exalted head, the Church and its members are already in communion with the Trinity; through its members it remains a part of the shattered communion of humankind. Indeed, this being the reality of the present state of the world, there is no other way in which the Church could be the Body of Christ, who emptied himself, assuming the nature of a slave. It is only because of its reaching into the farthest and most dismal parts of existence that the Church can be confident that it is the Body of Christ. The Church is 'sign, instrument and foretaste' of the kingdom precisely to the extent that it stands with Christ and the Holy Spirit as advocate for the helpless and the voiceless. More than that, it is frequently the case that the Spirit speaks to Christians through the 'other sheep' of Jesus, those not 'of this fold'. Within the kingdom of God, the earthly Church must always be attentive to the authentic voice of the Spirit, reminding of all that Jesus taught his first disciples, even when that voice appears to be speaking from outside the apparent boundaries of the Church. We say 'apparent' boundaries, because all creation, made and redeemed through the Word of God, must necessarily retain a relationship, however impaired, with the head and through the head with the members of the Church. All this needs to be remembered in a consideration of the Church as *koinonia*.

The Church as *koinonia*

The *koinonia* of the Church relates the Christian community directly to the communion of the Trinity and to God's mission to the whole of creation, and especially to those on the margins. Already in the New Testament, and in the writings of the early Fathers, the term is used in relation to the Church. It occurs in connection with the proclamation of the gospel and its associated invitation:

> We have seen it, and testify to it, and declare to you the eternal life that was with the Father and was revealed to us – we declare to you what we have seen and heard so that you also may have fellowship (*koinonia*) with us; and truly our fellowship (*koinonia*) is with the Father and with his Son Jesus Christ (1 John 1.2-3).

The idea also underlies many of the images used in the New Testament to portray the relationship of God's people to God and to one another: 'flock' (John 10.16); 'vine' (John 15.1); 'bride of Christ' (Revelation 21.2); 'body of Christ' (1 Corinthians 12.27); 'God's house' (Hebrews 3.1-6). Paul speaks of the relationship of believers to their Lord as 'being in Christ' (2 Corinthians 5.17), and of Christ being in the believer, through the indwelling of the Holy Spirit (Romans 8.1-11). In the twentieth century *koinonia* has been rediscovered as a particularly fruitful way of speaking of the nature and purpose of the Church. *Koinonia* is one of the most promising themes of contemporary ecumenical ecclesiology, resonating with contemplative experience, with a growing preference for personal over institutional ways of speaking about human relationships, and with contemporary concern for an ecological understanding of the place of humankind within creation as a whole. As a theme it has transformed the quest for visible unity and our approach to the structures which would best serve to maintain the Church's unity once this is understood primarily in relational and eschatological terms.

Jesus spoke of this communion in the great prayer of John 17: 'As you, Father, are in me, and I am in you, may they also be in us' (John 17.21). This is a personal and spiritual 'abiding' and it underlies both the salvation of the individual and the mission of the Church and all its members.

> The God whose being is holy love, uniting the Father, Son and Spirit, draws us by the work of the Spirit into participation in the Son's love and obedience to the Father . . . [In] that prayer in which Jesus consecrated himself as an offering to the Father, and in the same act consecrated his disciples to be offered in him, he also prayed that they might be kept in the same unity which binds him to the Father. Their corporate life is to be nothing less than a real participation in the life of the triune God – a life lived always in Christ and offered to the Father through the power of the Spirit. (*GROU: God's Reign and Our Unity*, paras 25, 27)

The Church enjoys already that eternal life which consists in knowing the only true God, and Jesus Christ whom he has sent (John 17.3). It participates in the light, love and life of the Holy Trinity of which the Johannine books of the New Testament speak. It is the 'blest communion, fellowship divine', in which Christians are united to Father, Son, and Holy Spirit, through all the means of grace (1 John 1.3,4,7) and to one another in and through that divine life. The Church tastes here and now 'the goodness of the word of God, and the powers of the age to come' (Hebrews 6.5), and rejoices in what it has already received. The Christ who has ascended high above all things is actually present in the world. The bride of Christ is already united with the bridegroom. The temple of God is filled with the presence of God. Christians rejoice, therefore, 'with an indescribable and glorious joy', even though they are still undergoing the process of reaping the harvest of their faith, that is the salvation of their souls (1 Peter 1.6-9).

But all this gives no grounds for triumphalism or arrogance. Indeed, with St Paul, if we must boast, we shall boast in the cross of Jesus Christ. That is the only basis for the authority of the Church to play its part in the saving work of God, because there is no other way of reconciliation. By initiation into a life of *koinonia* with God and with one another through faith and baptism, we are 'made one with Christ in his death and resurrection, to be cleansed and delivered from all sin' (ASB, Order for Baptism). The cross is the way to the kingdom of which *koinonia* is one of the central characteristics.

Although in its fullness *koinonia* is one of the marks of the heavenly church, it is also one of the indispensable marks of the Church *in via*. As such it refers not only to the means of grace by which God constantly sustains the Church, but also the quality of life which Christians should maintain in relation to each other and to the rest of the world for which Christ died. It is a principle of mutual belonging, which is highlighted, for example, in the Methodist ecclesiology of 'connexionalism', and which, albeit in different language, was a central feature of the *Dogmatic Constitution on the Church (Lumen Gentium)* of the Second Vatican Council.

This communion of baptized believers with Christ and with one another is expressed in a visible human community. It is a community called to live a Christ-like life, whose members participate in one another's joys and sorrows, and bear one another's burdens for the good of the whole (Philippians 2.1-5). There is mutual giving and receiving of spiritual and material goods, not only between individuals but also between communities, on the basis of a fellowship that already exists in Christ. In this communion, God is known to be all in all (Ephesians 1.23;3.19). It is the will of God for the whole creation that not only the Church, but all things should attain their unity and communion in Christ (Ephesians 1.10; 4.1-16). The Church, therefore, as communion, 'is sent into the world as sign, instrument and first fruits of a reality which comes from beyond history – the kingdom, or reign, of God' (*GROU*, para. 29).

2

How is the *Koinonia* of the Church Sustained for Service and Mission?

How is this journeying Church held together and sustained as a community 'on the way' so that it responds to God in love and praise and faithfully carries out God's mission in God's world? (Cf. ARCIC, *The Gift of Authority*, paras 34ff.) God, the Holy Trinity, is the source of the Church's life and gives to the Church all the gifts and resources needed for its life and for its mission. These gracious gifts maintain the Church in integrity as the Church of Christ and empower its ministry and its mission. They sustain the Church as the one, holy, catholic and apostolic Church. They provide a foretaste of the kingdom here and now. They enable the Church to be sign of the kingdom in the world. They empower the Church as instrument for the spread of God's kingdom.

The gift of the apostolic faith

Pre-eminent among the gifts of grace is the apostolic faith 'uniquely revealed in the Holy Scriptures' (Preface to the Declaration of Assent: Canon C15). The Scriptures of the Old and New Testaments are the divinely inspired witness to God's revelation, and the primary norm for Christian faith and life. Like the infant Christian community described in the Acts of the Apostles, the Church is to continue in the apostles' teaching (Acts 2.42). The faith of the Church from generation to generation is to be one with 'the faith that was once for all delivered to the saints' (Jude v.3).

The Church of England affirms that the apostolic faith is 'uniquely revealed in the Holy Scriptures and set forth in the catholic creeds, which faith the Church is called upon to proclaim afresh in each generation'. Living in the faith of the Church is a dynamic Spirit-filled and Spirit-led process. In each generation and in each place the Church is called to receive the apostolic faith, to live by it and to make it intelligible and relevant. The faith of the Church is constantly challenged by – and itself challenges – the culture of each place and each age. No one culture, no one period of history has a monopoly of insight into the faith of the Church. It is essential for the fullest apprehension of the faith to engage with Scripture, in prayer that is attentive to God, and to wait on the guidance of the Holy Spirit to lead into all truth. It is crucial for the fullest apprehension of the faith of the Apostles that the theological insights of different cultures and different ages are constantly brought together and interact. Sometimes the lived experience of one community in a particular time and place enables the faith to be perceived in new ways for the whole community. At other times, a desire for change or re-statement of the apostolic faith in one place provokes a crisis for the whole Church, revealing a need to explore, as an interpretative or hermeneutical community, what are the limits to diversity in the expression of the one faith. In the complexity of cultural contexts, synodical structures and ministries for taking counsel and deciding controversial matters are a crucial part of the life of the Church.

The Church's confession of the faith of the Apostles from generation to generation, both in the liturgical recitation of the Apostles' and Nicene-Constantinopolitan Creeds and in the theological exploration of Christian belief, is itself an act of the Church's trust in God and in God's providential care. It is an act of the Church inspired and sustained by the Holy Spirit as the Church lives in God's promise to lead the Church into all truth.

The Church witnesses to the special gift of apostolic faith by what it proclaims in word and deed; by how it serves the needs of its own people and the world; by how it seeks to include those on the margins and give voice to the voiceless. There is no authentic faith which, led by the Spirit, does not issue in care for all God's people and for God's creation.

The gift of the ministry of the word

Jesus inaugurated the Christian Church by proclaiming the good news of the kingdom of God (Mark 1.14-15) and brought the kingdom to birth by word and deed, by his death and resurrection. Similarly, the ministry of the word includes proclaiming the gospel of the cross and victory of Jesus

Christ by every possible appropriate means and expounding the canonical Scriptures to provide instruction in the faith. To preach the gospel of Christ, which is the power of God unto salvation (Romans 1.16), is a primary task of the Church and unites the Church in a common mission. With proclamation (*kerygma*) goes instruction (*didache*) for the building up of the faithful as the body of Christ (Ephesians 4.12). Both these tasks of the Church are expressions of its apostolicity, for the Church is apostolic when it is grounded in the apostolic proclamation and faithful to the apostolic mission.

The gift of the sacraments

Among the principal gifts of God's grace to strengthen the Church for its journey 'on the way' are the dominical sacraments of baptism and the Eucharist. The Scriptures are read and interpreted in the celebration of the sacraments. The apostolic faith is encountered in the hearing of the word and in the experience of the sacraments. In the sacrament of baptism Christians die and rise again with Christ, through the waters of baptism, to new life in him. In the Eucharist they encounter the central mysteries of the apostolic faith in the *anamnesis*, the making present of those past events. They experience the future glory, here and now, through the power of the Spirit.

Baptism is the fundamental sacrament of initiation into the body of Christ and thus into the *koinonia* of the Church. Baptism consists of the sacramental action with the element of water and the accompanying trinitarian confession of the apostolic faith. Christians are united through their baptism with Christ in his death and resurrection (Romans 6.3-11) and brought into a covenantal union with him (Galatians 3.26-29).

> Through baptism, Christians are brought into union with Christ, with each other and with the Church of every time and place. Our common baptism, which unites us to Christ in faith, is thus a basic bond of unity. (*BEM: Baptism, Eucharist and Ministry*, B6)

Baptism brings with it responsibility to live as a child of God, an inheritor of the kingdom of heaven, to witness to God's love and to serve the needs of the Church and the world. Those baptized are called as individuals and together to reflect the glory of the Lord, transformed by the power of the Holy Spirit into the likeness of Christ. The life of the baptized is one of continuing struggle and continuing renewal through the experience of grace.

As the baptized grow in the life of faith they demonstrate that by God's grace humanity can be regenerated and liberated. They have a shared responsibility to witness together to the apostolic faith and to minister to the needs of the Church and the world.

> Baptism into Christ's death has ethical implications which not only call for personal sanctification, but also motivate Christians to strive for the realization of the will of God in all realms of life (Romans 6.9ff., Galatians 3.27-28; 1 Peter 2.21–4.6). (*BEM* B10)

In the Eucharist the *koinonia* with God and with each other, first given in baptism, is sustained, enhanced and drawn towards eschatological perfection (1 Corinthians 11.26) as Christ, by the power of the Holy Spirit, gives himself to God's people. There is a dynamic connection between baptism, as the fundamental sacrament of initiation into the body of Christ, and the Eucharist in which the life of the Church as a divine communion is expressed most clearly. The gift of communion (*koinonia*) given in baptism is brought to expression in the Eucharist. The sharing in one bread and the partaking in one cup in a given place and time demonstrate and effect the unity of those who share it in a particular time and place with those who share it in all times and places. 'In the local church the Eucharist is the fundamental expression of the walking together (synodality) of the people of God' (ARCIC, *The Gift of Authority*, para. 36).

Baptism, Eucharist and Ministry expresses in a powerful way the fundamental relation between the Eucharist and all aspects of life:

> The eucharistic celebration demands reconciliation and sharing amongst all those regarded as brothers and sisters in the one family of God and is a constant challenge in the search for appropriate relationships in social, economic and political life (Matthew 5.23ff.; 1 Corinthians 10.16ff.; 1 Corinthians 11.20-22, Galatians 3.28). All kinds of injustice, racism, separation and lack of freedom are radically challenged when we share in the body and blood of Christ. Through the eucharist the all-renewing grace of God penetrates and restores human personality and dignity. The eucharist involves the

believer in the central event of the world's history. As participants in the eucharist, therefore, we prove inconsistent if we are not actively participating in this ongoing restoration of the world's situation and the human condition. The eucharist shows us that our behaviour is inconsistent in face of the reconciling presence of God in human history; we are placed under continual judgement by the persistence of unjust relationships of all kinds in our society, the manifold divisions on account of human pride, material interest and power politics and, above all, the obstinacy of unjustifiable confessional opposition within the body of Christ. (*BEM* E20)

The gift of apostolic ministry

All the faithful, who are baptized into the life and love of God, Father, Son and Holy Spirit, are given a charism of the Holy Spirit for the building up of the body of Christ, the Church, and for the service of the world. The calling of the people of God (*laos*) is lived out in a broad context of social and community life in civil society – at work, in recreation and within the family as well as within the life of the parish and sometimes in the service of the Church at diocesan or regional level. By virtue of their baptism all members are called to confess the apostolic faith of the Church, and to give account of the hope that is in them.

It is the calling of all baptized believers to represent Christ and his Church; to bear witness to him wherever they may be; and, according to the gifts given to them by his Holy Spirit, to carry out Christ's work of reconciliation in the world.

To enable the entire community of faith to respond to Christ's call, God has given to the Church the charism of ordered ministry, a single ministry ordered in the most ancient form in the episcopate, the presbyterate and the diaconate. The ordained ministry is exercised with, in and among the whole people of God. From the earliest days, the ministry of the word and the celebration of the sacraments were understood as the central responsibility of those called to exercise oversight, as a primary means of equipping the whole community for its ministry of service and mission. That responsibility is given by God and entrusted by the community in the act of ordination.

In episcopally ordered churches, bishops, as chief pastors, have a particular concern for the unity and the *koinonia* of the Church:

> [A]s a chief pastor [the bishop] shares with his fellow bishops a special responsibility to maintain and further the unity of the Church, to uphold its discipline and guard the faith. (*The Ordinal of the Church of England*, ASB,1980)

The Cameron Report, *Episcopal Ministry*, describes the bishop's ministry of unity and continuity as exercised in the 'three planes of the Church's life'. The first plane is that of the 'local church' or diocese. Here the bishop is a 'focus of the community's worship and life, and in protecting it as guardian of its faith and order, the bishop stands in a relationship to the community, which makes it possible for him to act on its behalf'.

The second plane of the Church's life is that of the Church catholic or universal. In keeping contact and communication with the leaders of other worshipping communities on his people's behalf, the bishop has been the person, in every age, who has held together the local community with other Christian communities. Through the ordination of deacons and presbyters into catholic order and especially through the consecration of bishops, Christian communities remain constantly in touch with one another throughout the Church. So the bishop holds in unity the local church with every other local church with which it is in communion.

The third or apostolic plane of the Church's life is the continuity of the life of the Church in time, from the apostles to the present day. The primary manifestation of apostolic succession is the fidelity of the whole Church to the apostolic teaching and mission. The succession of bishops from generation to generation 'was understood as serving, symbolizing and guarding the continuity of the apostolic faith and communion'. Within the apostolic continuity of the whole Church and all its means of grace, the succession of bishops 'is a sign of assurance to the faithful that the Church remains in continuity with the Apostles' teaching and mission'.

Bishops share their ministry of care for the communion of the Church in a special way with the presbyters they ordain and license. 'A priest is called by God to work with the bishop and his fellow priests as servant and shepherd among the people to whom he is sent' (*ASB Ordinal*). In services of institution this is expressed by the bishop in the words: 'receive this cure which is both yours and mine'.

Deacons, while not sharing the ministry of the bishop in the presidency of word and sacrament, do work in close association with the bishop in the ministry of pastoral care and service in the community. Ordination and licensing establishes the integral relationship between bishop and deacon as between bishop and presbyter.

Summary

God's gracious gifts of the apostolic faith (uniquely revealed in the Holy Scriptures), the apostolic ministry of word and sacrament and the many other charisms of ministry sustain the *koinonia* of the Church. They connect the Church in every place and every time, maintaining the unity and continuity of the Church. They equip the Church for carrying on Christ's mission in the world. The Anglican Communion, in its adherence to the Lambeth Quadrilateral, understands the characteristics of Scriptures, creeds, sacraments and the historic episcopate to be fundamental for the unity and *koinonia* of the Church. This was reaffirmed by the bishops of the Anglican Communion at the 1998 Lambeth Conference (Resolution IV. 2).

These gifts provide the means for the local churches (dioceses) to live in communion with each other in the present and in continuity with the Church through the ages. They are gifts providing connectedness. They make possible a dynamic and united life of the community of faith, a life that responds to the challenges of the contemporary world, seeking to engage with those on the margins of the life of the Church and endeavouring to witness to those who have not heard the gospel message.

3

Collegiality in the Context of Conciliarity and Primacy

From the earliest times, God's gift of a ministry of pastoral oversight (*episkope*) has sustained the Church in proclaiming the faith in changing circumstances and in building up the life of the Christian community 'on the way'. The whole community is charged with living the gospel and witnessing to God's mission of reconciliation for all. The apostolic ministry of oversight is given by God to sustain the community in that task. The Ordinal in the *Alternative Service Book* says: 'A bishop is called to lead in serving and caring for the people of God and to work with them in the oversight of the Church.'

Here the Ordinal highlights the relational character of the ministry of oversight which entails a mutual responsibility between *episkopoi* and the whole apostolic community of the Church. This means that the responsibility of those called to exercise oversight in the Church cannot be fulfilled without the collaboration, support and assent of the community. At the same time the effective and faithful life of the community is served by a set-apart ministry of leadership in mission, teaching and the common life focused by the sacraments.

Representative ministry

The Church is commissioned to represent Christ. Through his Church, though not only so, Christ is present in the world. All its members are called to discern and witness to his presence (Matthew 18.18-20). The mission of God in the sending of Jesus Christ and the mission of the Church on behalf of Jesus Christ are one mission. When, in the high-priestly prayer of John 17, Jesus prays for his disciples, he seems to include also all whom the Father has given him, all whom he has loved and for whose sake he sanctifies himself to the cross that they may all behold his glory. His commission is, therefore, not restricted to the Twelve, but

14

embraces all who are his own. 'As you have sent me into the world, so I have sent them into the world' (John 17.18). The commission of the risen Christ in John 20.21ff. is given to the disciples as representative of the whole Church. Christ gives them authority and power to speak and act on his behalf and thus to represent him in their mission. 'As the Father has sent me, so I send you . . . Receive the Holy Spirit' (John 20.21-22). Is it not all those who have received the Holy Spirit – all baptized believers – who are sent into the world to witness? Through faith and baptism Christians are united with Christ. Their Christ-centred identity means that all Christians, when living out their calling, represent Christ to others. All have a ministry or form of service (1 Corinthians 12.4-11). All represent Christ and his Church by virtue of their baptism which has united them to Christ in his death and resurrection. All the baptized believers are *in persona Christi*. They carry Christ in their hearts and witness to him in their lives. The momentum of Christian spirituality and mission stems from the fact that the baptized live, speak and act for Christ. They are individually members of his body and temples of the Holy Spirit (1 Corinthians 6.19).

Representativeness is thus a principle that applies to the whole Church. It transcends the distinction in calling between the laity and the ordained, since all members of the apostolic community, the Church, are called to represent Christ, to be his ambassadors, to speak and act in his name. It is to the seventy-two as well as to the Twelve that Jesus says: 'He who welcomes/receives/listens to you welcomes/receives/listens to me and him who sent me' (Matthew 10.1,40; Luke 10.1,16; cf. John 13.20; cf. Paul's apostolic ambassadorship: 2 Corinthians 5.20). Clergy and laity share a common fundamental calling, a partnership with one another in Christ (Hebrews 3.1,14).

The apostolic ministry is, however, representative of Christ and the Church in a special way. 2 Corinthians 4 – 5 is an extended exposition of the responsibilities of apostolic ministry and the authority that undergirds it. The Anglican – Reformed dialogue expresses it thus:

> The minister as leader has a representative character, to act as 'the one on behalf of the many', so that the whole Church is represented in his person as he carries on his heart the concerns of all his people. He does not act in his own name, but in the name of Christ, and in

the name of the whole body of Christ, so that he is at once the mouthpiece of our Lord and the mouthpiece of his flock. (*GROU*, para. 85)

The principle of representativeness, therefore, is fundamental to the life and mission of the Church and in a particular way the apostolic ministry is charged to represent Christ to the Church and to the world. In episcopal churches:

> Bishops and presbyters represent both Christ and his people in their leadership of the Church and its mission, in the proclamation of the Gospel, in the articulation of faith, and in the celebration of the sacraments. (*The Priesthood of the Ordained Ministry*, para. 144)

The representative ministry of the bishop is seen particularly in the bishop's role as the principal minister of the sacraments in the local church or diocese and, therefore, president of the Eucharist within the diocese. The Eucharist, which always comprises word and sacrament, is a sign of the unity of the local church/diocese and of its communion with all the local churches/dioceses around the world and through time, and it is a foretaste of the heavenly banquet. As the bishop is both chief pastor of the local church and a member of the universal college of pastors, the bishop is the personal focus of communion between the local church and other churches.

The existence of a representative ministry entails a responsibility both of those who represent and those who are represented. Those who represent the community have a duty to listen to the community, to discern the mind of Christ in conversation with the local community, and in conversation with all local communities today and through the ages. They are called to seek always that which is in conformity with the normative witness of Holy Scripture. At the same time those who are represented are called to receive with attentiveness and respect the teaching of those set in leadership over them, with whom they stand in a relationship of critical solidarity. A representative ministry implies mutual responsibilities and mutual accountability in order that the whole Church may remain faithful to the gospel entrusted to it.

Within the life of the Christian community there is a proper place for obedience. The author of the Letter to the Hebrews writes:

> Obey your leaders and submit to them, for they are keeping watch over your souls and will give an account. Let them do this with joy and not with sighing – for that would be harmful to you. (Hebrews 13.17)

This injunction is set within a call for the people to remember their leaders, 'those who spoke the word of God to you; consider the outcome of their way of life, and imitate their faith' (Hebrews 13.7). Within the ordained ministry too, obedience is required. In the *Ordinal of the Book of Common Prayer* the bishop says to the deacon 'Will you reverently obey your Ordinary, and other chief Ministers of the Church, and them to whom government over you is committed?' The same obedience is required of those the bishop ordains as priests. The bishop himself owes 'due obedience' to his metropolitan.

It is the authority of Christ which is entrusted to those who exercise a representative ministry in the Church for the sake of the unity, holiness, apostolicity and catholicity of the Church. Authority is the authority of the crucified Lord – the one who came to serve and not to be served.

In the diocese the minister with oversight exercises leadership in manifold ways: in mission; in the ministry of the word and sacraments; in worship, prayer and praise; in guardianship of the faith; in the declaration of the forgiveness of sins to those who turn to God in repentance and faith; and in discipline. And the minister of oversight has special responsibilities in commissioning for ministry in the Church on behalf of Christ and his people.

Oversight in the specific areas of leadership, consultation and discernment, and decision-making is also a vital aspect of the Church's life. It is integrally related to the ministry of the word, the administration of the sacraments and the provision of primary pastoral care, holding them together and facilitating their enactment. Oversight belongs in a special way to those ordained but it is exercised within, and in relation to, the whole Church:

> Responsibility for the maintenance of the apostolic faith is shared by the whole people of God. Every Christian has a part in this responsibility. The task of those entrusted with oversight, acting in the name of Christ, is to foster the prompting of the Spirit and to keep the community within the bounds of the apostolic faith, to sustain and

> promote the Church's mission, by preaching, explaining and apply-
> ing the truth. In responding to the insights of the community, and of
> the individual Christian, whose conscience is also moulded by the
> same Spirit, those exercising oversight seek to discern what is the
> mind of Christ. Discernment involves both heeding and sifting in
> order to assist the people of God in understanding, articulating and
> applying the faith. Sometimes an authoritative expression has to be
> given to the insights and convictions of the faithful. The community
> actively responds to the teaching of the ordained ministry, and when,
> under the guidance of the Spirit, it recognises the apostolic faith, it
> assimilates its content into its life. (ARCIC, *Church as Communion*,
> para. 32)

In different ways churches have sought to return to what they variously
understood to be an apostolic church order so as to maintain the apostolicity of the Church. Some churches, while maintaining an apostolic
ministry of oversight, abandoned the form and sign of episcopal order.
Others maintained episcopacy, though with a 'temporary' break in the
form and sign of succession, while another group, like the Church of
England, continued the episcopal form and sign of succession within the
tradition of the catholic Church. The result of this fragmentation of the
universal Church has been the loss of a single ministry of oversight in the
service of the *koinonia* of the whole Church and its mission.

Personal, collegial and communal

In recent years theological dialogues, bilateral and multilateral, have
devoted much attention to the question of the ministry of *episkope* (oversight). There is a growing ecumenical consensus that *episkope* is necessary
to express and safeguard the unity of the body of Christ and to serve its
mission.

> Every church needs the ministry of unity in some form in order to be
> the Church of God, the one body of Christ, a sign of the unity of all
> in the Kingdom. (*BEM*, M23)

Baptism, Eucharist and Ministry further states that 'the ordained ministry
should be exercised in a personal, collegial and communal way' and that
this pattern operates 'at every level of the Church's life'.

It should be *personal* because the presence of Christ among his people can most effectively be pointed to by the person ordained to proclaim the Gospel and to call the community to serve the Lord in unity of life and witness. It should also be *collegial*, for there is need for a college of ordained ministers sharing in the common task of representing the concerns of the community. Finally, the intimate relationship between the ordained ministry and the community should find expression in a communal dimension where the exercise of the ordained ministry is rooted in the life of the community and requires the community's effective participation in the discovery of God's will and the guidance of the Spirit. (*BEM*, M26)

Although in *Baptism, Eucharist and Ministry* this threefold pattern is applied to ordained ministry generally, our task here, in exploring the theology of collegiality, requires us to apply it particularly to the ministry of bishops – to the communal, collegial and personal dimensions of episcopal ministry.

The emphasis on the personal, collegial and communal dimensions makes clear the fundamentally collaborative nature of *episkope* in the Church. The personal, collegial and communal ways of working can be discerned in the preaching of the gospel, the administration of the sacraments and pastoral oversight. The care of the Church involves the structural exercise of authority in leadership, consultation, discernment, and decision-making. While the pastoral aspect of oversight is perhaps mostly exercised in the personal mode, the exercise of authority in leadership, consultation, discernment, and decision-making is carried out predominantly in the collegial and communal modes. Authority in the Church requires consent. Leadership needs followers who are willing to accept the lead that is offered. Consultation by definition involves other parties. And decision-making demands that those who will be affected by a decision are involved in making it. The whole Church is involved in this communal dimension of *episkope*. 'The perception of God's will for his Church does not belong only to the ordained ministry but is shared by all its members.' (ARCIC, *Final Report, Authority 1*, p. 54, para. 6)

The three dimensions – personal, collegial, communal – need to be kept together. However, as *Baptism, Eucharist and Ministry* says, in various churches one or another has been overemphasized at the expense of the others. In some churches, the personal dimension of the ordained ministry tends to diminish the collegial and communal dimensions. In other churches, the collegial and communal dimension takes so much importance that the ordained ministry loses the personal dimension. Each church, including our own, needs to ask itself in what way its exercise of ordained ministry has become unbalanced in the course of history (*BEM*, M26c).

Confusion over terminology

The language used to speak of the different dimensions of the ministry of oversight differs between churches, even between theologians in the same church, and between ecumenical reports. This causes misunderstanding in conducting the debate on the ministry of oversight. The terms **communal**, **conciliar** and **synodal** describe a quality of the ongoing life of the whole body of the Church and not merely particular structures and processes which serve its ongoing life.

The word **personal** is also commonly used in a variety of ways. When the word personal is used in relation to the ministry of oversight it does not refer to an individualistic exercise of independent or autocratic leadership. Even when a bishop apparently acts as an individual (personally), or as a member of the episcopal college (collegially), his authority and the manner in which it is exercised always derives from his relation to Christ, to the Church through the ages and to the contemporary Church which he is consecrated to serve.

A confusion also relates to the term **collegial**. Mindful of the origins of the paper, we focus upon the use of the terms collegial and collegiality in relation to the collegiality of bishops, though we acknowledge that it is often used of other groupings, particularly of the relation between a bishop and his presbyters. The collegiality of bishops may be applied both to the permanent order and ministry of the episcopate as such, and also to special gatherings of bishops, called together for particular tasks.

The personal, the collegial and the communal (synodal or conciliar) belong together. It would be appropriate to take them in any order for any one implies and involves the other two. Nevertheless, we have chosen to begin with the conciliar (communal or synodal), and then to move on to the personal and finally to the collegial.

Communal

The communal (conciliar or synodal) life of the Church is grounded in the sacrament of baptism. All the baptized share a responsibility for the apostolic faith and witness of the Church. Conciliarity refers to the involvement of the whole body of the faithful – bishops, clergy and laity – in consultation, normally through representative and constitutional structures, for the sake of the well-being of the Church and God's mission in the world. Conciliar life sustains all the baptized in a web of belonging, of mutual accountability and support. Its nature is fundamentally eucharistic (ARCIC, *The Gift of Authority*, para. 39). It implies unity in diversity and is expressed in one heart and one mind among Christians (Philippians 2.1-2). It is the way Christians are held together in unity, local churches travel together as the one Church and the one Church is manifested in the life of each local church. Conciliarity is the way of being the Church which enables the whole Christian community to discern the mind of Christ.

This conciliarity lies behind the Anglican conviction that authority in the Church is dispersed and corporate and entails processes of discernment and moments of articulation. In these processes there has to be an ongoing dialogue, within the single community of the Church, between those entrusted with a personal ministry of oversight and all the baptized members of the royal priesthood. This is one of the consequences of a personal ministry which is representative – both of Christ to the community and of the community to itself, and to its Lord. Within a constitutional and representative understanding of church government, bishops have a special, though not isolated, responsibility. Throughout history, the way this responsibility has been exercised has developed and changed.

The conciliar life of the Church was perhaps first expressed and focused in the Council of Jerusalem (Acts 15) where the apostles and elders, presided over by James, reached a common mind on a matter affecting the fundamental unity of the Church. Of the decision reached in the Council, the Church could say: 'It has seemed good to the Holy Spirit and to us' (Acts

15.28). The conciliar life of the apostolic Church, reflected in the Council of Jerusalem, was not only the event itself but also the discernment that led up to it and the reception of it that followed in the life of the Church (cf. the witness of the Epistle to the Galatians). Prior to the calling of the Council there was discussion of the conditions for the entry of the Gentiles into the community. Following the Council there was a need for a process of reception of the decision of the Council in the life of local communities.

The New Testament in Acts 15 demonstrates the need for the community, with its leaders, to be gathered together to discern matters concerning the faith and life of the Church. This early experience of conciliar life was carried further in the second and third centuries as bishops and other representatives of the Church in particular regions met together to resolve potentially church-dividing issues such as the date of Easter, the challenge of heresy and the problem of those who lapsed during persecution. These provincial councils, which from the outset involved some participation of laity as well as clergy, were concerned not only with the internal life of the region, but also with the unity of the whole Church.

The conversion of Constantine provided the political framework in which potentially ecumenical councils (i.e. councils that were representative of the universal Church) could be called together. Ecumenical councils were convened to maintain the Church in fidelity to the apostolic witness and to speak for the entire Christian community. From the apostolic age onwards the Church experienced serious conflicts of interpretation of the faith, and through the medium of synods, found it possible to make decisions on the authentic form of doctrine and practice (cf. *Towards a Church of England Response to BEM and ARCIC*, para. 223). In making such judgements, synods understood their decisions to be consonant with, or taken out of Scripture, even when, as at Nicea in 325 or at Chalcedon in 451, they found it impossible, if grave heresy was to be excluded, merely to repeat the words of Scripture. Beyond the declaration, a council's decision had to be received by the whole Church:

> [A]lthough it is not through reception by the people of God that a definition first acquires authority, the assent of the faithful is the ultimate indication that the Church's authoritative decision in a matter of faith has been truly preserved from error by the Holy Spirit.

> The Holy Spirit who maintains the Church in the truth will bring its members to receive the definition as true and to assimilate it if what has been declared genuinely expounds the revelation. (ARCIC, *Final Report, Authority II*, para. 25)

Later, following the division between East and West, the conciliar movement in the West developed in response to a protracted crisis of authority in the Church. The councils of the early fifteenth century (Pisa, Constance and Basel) were examples of this form of conciliar activity before the Reformation. Conciliar thought held that authority resides in the whole Church and is articulated by general and provincial councils. It promoted the principles of representativeness, constitutionalism and consent. There was, however, a growing tendency in this period to oppose the authority of the whole Church expressed in councils to primatial (i.e. papal) authority. This episode illustrates the constant danger in the life of the Church of separating the personal exercise of oversight from its exercise within, and in relation to, the conciliar life of the whole Church.

These conciliar developments coincided with the rise of national identities and aspirations. The Reformers, both Continental and English, affirmed the conciliar principle and appealed for a free general council to deal with the divisions of the Church. The Reformers welcomed the contribution of scholars and gave an increased formal role to lay people. In England the role of Parliament and the Royal Supremacy ensured that the laity was involved in the governance of the Church of England. One negative consequence of the sixteenth-century divisions was the further entrenchment of the Church's inability, both bishops and representative lay people, to meet together in general council for guarding the faith of the Church.

In the post-Reformation period, Anglican divines continued to promote conciliar ecclesiology. The expansion of the Church of England overseas, partly as a result of British colonization, led to the formation of many new Anglican provinces, each eventually provided with its own synodical structures for maintaining the life of the Church in a particular place and time. In the post-colonial period of the twentieth century, the various interdependent Anglican churches have come to be governed by synods which recognize the authority of the episcopate as crucial and distinct, but which include not only presbyteral but also lay representation. However, the form of conciliar structure is not identical in each Anglican province. The local context plays a part in shaping the different provincial structures and processes.

In the Anglican Communion today there is no legislative authority wider than the provincial/national level. Nevertheless, there has been a growing realization that, to maintain communion effectively, the conciliar life of the Communion needs wider structures and processes. Both the personal ministry of the Archbishop of Canterbury and the collegiality of the Lambeth Conference serve the *koinonia* of the Anglican Communion. The involvement of the wider fellowship of episcopally ordered churches in communion and of ecumenical partners keeps the Anglican Communion open to the potentially worldwide fellowship of the Church.

The Anglican Consultative Council, established by a resolution of the 1968 Lambeth Conference, brings together every three years bishops, presbyters and laity, under the presidency of the Archbishop of Canterbury. It is not and never could take the place of an ecumenical council. Nevertheless, while there is division in the universal Church, it serves, together with the Lambeth Conference, as a reminder of the conciliar expression of the one Church. The presence of churches in communion and ecumenical guests keeps Anglicans mindful of the promise of greater unity. As *The Virginia Report* says:

> Its most vital purpose, however, like the Lambeth Conference, is to establish a communion of mutual attentiveness, interdependence and accountability to serve the unity and interdependence in mission of the Anglican Communion. The mutual attentiveness required when members from various parts of the Communion share the richness of their experiences also helps to form the mind of the Communion and is a reminder of the rich diversity of gifts which God has given us. The sharing of stories enhances and deepens the Communion's experience of interdependence at all levels.

> Important to this process are representatives who are able not only to bring the concerns and stories of their Provinces with them but carry the proceedings of the council back to their communities, at the Provincial, national and diocesan levels. Only this constant inter-

change will provide the basis on which member Churches are able to develop and maintain constant relations and full communion with their sisters and brothers around the world. Each Provincial Church has a responsibility to assist their representatives to carry out this task. (*Virginia Report*, 3.43 & 3.44)

The report of the 1948 Lambeth Conference stresses that the sources of authority in Anglicanism are dispersed rather than centralized. They are distributed among Scripture, tradition, creeds, the ministry of the word and sacraments, the witness of saints, and the *consensus fidelium*, which is the Holy Spirit acting among and through his faithful people.

Thus the clues to correct teaching and right judgement are gleaned from the numerous and diverse sources, distributed in the wisdom of God. This suggests that a patient, prayerful and prolonged process of education, discernment and reception is required. The Church, including the bishops corporately and individually, is constantly engaged in this task. The stress that the Lambeth 1948 Conference placed upon the consensus of the faithful is consonant with the conciliar tradition. The statement goes on to point out that there is a God-given purpose in the dispersed nature of authority in the Church:

It is thus a dispersed rather than a centralised authority having many elements which combine, interact with, and check each other; these elements together contributing by a process of mutual support, mutual checking, and redressing of errors or exaggerations to the many-sided fullness of the authority which Christ has committed to his Church. Where this authority of Christ is to be found mediated not in one mode but in several we recognise in this multiplicity God's loving provision against the temptations to tyranny and the dangers of unchecked power. (*Lambeth Conference 1948*, p. 84)

Conciliarity refers both to institutional structures and to the processes, within and beyond those structures that maintain the Church in a life of communion. Without a system of conciliar structures beyond the local, there is a risk of communion being sacrificed to local preoccupations. At the same time, a conciliar structure which does not take to heart the integrity and concerns of the local risks sacrificing local diversity in favour of general uniformity. Conciliarity, with its principle of dispersed authority, acknowledges the frailty and fallibility of human nature. Conciliarity enables the Church to assimilate insights from many sources and to be open to prophetic witness. It is open in principle to criticism and correction. Conciliar authority reflects the deep wisdom of Christian experience. It recognizes that there is a limit to the amount of responsibility one person or group of people can be expected to bear for the spiritual welfare of many others. It lightens the burdens of Christian leaders by placing their distinctive ministry within the economy of the whole body. While true conciliarity militates against short-term changes of policy, it ensures that when change is required, it will be well thought-out and enjoy widespread support.

Personal

Conciliarity stands for the involvement of the whole Church, as the body of Christ, in taking responsibility for the faithful life and mission of the Church. This does not detract from the responsibility of each individual Christian for the faith into which he or she is baptized, nor from that of the representative leaders of the community who are given responsibility to maintain, guard and interpret the faith and to lead in mission.

The ministry of oversight should be personal because when someone is ordained to proclaim the gospel and to call the community to faithfulness, he or she points to the presence of Christ among his people (see *BEM*, M26). Bishops have a special responsibility for maintaining and focusing the internal unity and communion of the local church. In the dioceses where they have oversight they represent, focus and care for the unity of the Church. Bishops also relate the local church to the wider Church and the wider Church back to the local church. Just as this personal dimension of ministry is fundamental to the conciliar life of the Church, so it is vital for collegiality. The collegiality of bishops is nothing if it is not a sharing in a common ministry by persons called and ordained to oversee the conciliar life and the mission of the Church.

Personal oversight is not an individual ministry. 'Persons' are not to be understood apart from their connection with the community. Bishops, like all Christians, are called to follow Christ the servant, who set his disciples an example by washing their feet (John 13.14-15). They are dependent upon the grace of God, through the power of the Holy Spirit bestowed in Christ Jesus. They receive the anointing of the same Spirit, who animates the life of all believers, and are inseparably bound to them. They should not be exalted above the community, but should point to the unique mediatorial role of Christ and not to themselves.

There is an aspect of the personal dimension of ordained ministry that bears upon the unity of the episcopal college and on the coherence of the conciliar life of the Church. Primacy is an expression of *BEM's* 'personal' mode of ministry. Primacy needs both collegiality and conciliarity so that it may be representative in its actions and constitutional in its exercise of authority. Given that, primacy can strengthen the unity of the Church and enable the Church to speak with one voice.

Anglicans operate with a principle of primacy in several areas. Primacy is local, provincial and – potentially – worldwide. The diocesan bishop is the chief pastor, principal minister of the sacraments and ordinary in his diocese. The Archbishops of Canterbury and York exercise a primatial role in their respective provinces (where they have visitatorial powers and authority in appeals), and jointly in the General Synod of the Church of England (as its Presidents). The Archbishop of Canterbury, additionally, has a primatial role in the Anglican Communion where he presides at the Lambeth Conference and has a pastoral ministry to the Anglican bishops.

Anglicans are not unreceptive to the principle of a universal ministry in the service of unity that respects the integrity of local churches and acknowledges the authority of the whole body of bishops, clergy and laity expressed through conciliar channels. The Church of England has recently considered this idea in *May They All Be One: A Response of the House of Bishops of the Church of England to* Ut Unum Sint.

Primacy in this sense is a particular form of the exercise of personal oversight. As such, it must always be set within the framework of consultation and consent which is fundamental to the right exercise of authority in the Church.

Collegial

Christ's commission in the New Testament is to his apostles as a body and to the Church as represented by them. Just as the personal exercise of oversight safeguards the conciliar from being collective, so the collegial safeguards the personal from being individualistic. Bishops exercise individually a ministry which is shared by them as a body; collegiality is implicit in the nature of the ministry of oversight. We have already noted that the existence of a representative ministry entails a responsibility both on those who represent and on those who are represented (cf. p. 16). This is especially worth emphasizing under the heading of collegiality. Individual bishops, as representative persons, have a duty to exercise oversight in their diocese in a manner that accords with the principle of conciliarity, sharing their responsibilities, in appropriate ways, with presbyters and elected lay people. They consult through synodical and other channels and encourage the local church (diocese) as a whole, and in every constituent part (parishes), to take responsibility for its life. In this way they enable the body of Christ to realize its true nature, and to release its energies for mission to the world. Equally the college of bishops must exercise its proper oversight in a particular province/national church in accordance with the same principle. They will take seriously the notes of encouragement or warning that emerge from synodical discussion, carry the whole Church with them, as far as possible, by patient education and steadfast example when controversial issues have to be resolved, and maintain an open boundary to sources of insight and inspiration from outside the episcopate. At the same time, the body of the faithful, understanding the relationship to the whole Church in which they stand (by baptism and through the ministry of the episcopal college), will accept the restraint implicit in that relationship. Local perceptions and loyalties (whether understood chronologically or geographically) must take their place within the discipline of the One Body. The solidarity between the college of bishops and the body of the faithful is, as we have said (p. 16), a 'critical solidarity'; the Spirit leads the people of God into all truth. But as the process of discernment and reception proceeds towards the *consensus fidelium*, the faithful will bring to it a predisposition to expect that the guidance they receive from their Fathers in God is 'trustworthy and true'.

Collegiality reflects the fact that all bishops have received the same ministry through their ordination as bishops. They are guardians of the same faith and overseers in the one Church. This is as true of the individual bishop as the chief pastor of his particular diocese (in which the whole Church is manifested) as it is of the episcopate when it meets together to take counsel and offer leadership to the Church at wider levels, whether regionally or worldwide. Collegiality issues in the corporate, representative exercise of oversight. This involves leadership, consultation, discernment and decision-making. It brings together the personal and relational in the exercise of leadership and authority. Collegiality is clearly seen at work wherever those entrusted with leadership and authority in the Church speak and act as one. Episcopal collegiality is particularly clearly expressed when bishops who have jurisdiction in the local church meet together to care for the unity and fidelity of the whole Church. Collegiality entails:

> [S]eeking as one body the wisdom and insight that come from the grace of God's Holy Spirit in and through corporate prayer and reflection, and expressing to the rest of the Church and to the world the common mind given to them as a result. (*The Nature of Christian Belief*, 1986, para. 64)

Enabling the Church to conform to the mind of Christ is a continuous process involving the whole community. Within this process the college of bishops has a special role in keeping the Church true to the apostolic teaching and mission. In doing so it draws upon insights which come from corporate prayer, study and reflection in which Scripture, tradition and reason each play a part. In this way the wisdom and experience of all the Christian communities and of the contemporary world is brought to bear on the oversight of the Church. Collegiality entails ensuring that different voices are heard in discussion, listening to expert opinion and drawing on appropriate sources of scholarship.

> One important way in which bishops can fulfil their task is by helping the Church to benefit from the work of professional scholars. The whole people of God needs the wider resources of different communities of knowledge, and the rigour and self-criticism of the academic world. Among those who teach in our universities and other centres

> of higher education there are many Christian men and women
> whose integrity of mind and spirit, exercised in lives of faith and
> prayer, makes an indispensable contribution to the wider Church . . .
> Bishops both collegially and individually, are well placed . . . to draw
> on such teachers . . . and to help interpret the work of scholars
> creatively into the prayer and thought and life of the Christian
> community at large. (*The Nature of Christian Belief*, para. 69)

In the process of enabling the Church to conform to the mind of Christ,
the college has a duty to prevent the premature closure of debate and to
encourage the waiting upon the guidance of the Holy Spirit. Episcopal
collegiality helps the Church to live with a degree of theological
provisionality as the will of Christ for his Church is being discerned.
It involves the delicate and complex task of making room for those of
different opinions while guarding and promoting unity – that is to say,
helping the Church to discern the tolerable limits to diversity in issues of
faith, order and morals by giving moral and spiritual leadership. Speaking
collegially does not mean speaking in full agreement on every subject. An
agreed statement may reflect the diversity of opinion and dilemmas that
exist within the Church at any particular place and time. For example,
although the majority of the Church of England supports its decision
to ordain women, there remains a substantial minority opposed. This
diversity is represented in the House of Bishops. The House of Bishops
therefore produced *The Manchester Statement* setting out a framework for
the oversight of those opposed to women's ordination during a period of
open reception within the Church of England, the Anglican Communion
and the universal Church. Collegiality serves *koinonia* when the unity of
the Church is threatened as well as when consensus is more apparent.

Collegiality entails mutual responsibility and accountability between
those who are members of the episcopal college. As representative
persons:

> Bishops . . . have to work under a discipline of mutual responsibility
> and accountability, and to be sensitive to traditional beliefs within the
> Church as well as to fresh insights. A bishop may properly enter into
> questioning on matters of belief, both because as a man of integrity
> he will feel any force there is in such questionings, and also because

as a leader part of his responsibility on behalf of the Church is to listen honestly to criticisms of its faith and life. But in all he says he must take care not to present variant beliefs as if they were the faith of the Church; and he must always make as sure as he can that his hearers understand what that faith is and the reasons for it. (*The Nature of Christian Belief,* para. 70)

Episcopal collegiality also benefits from a shared ministry between the bishops and the other ordained ministers in a diocese. *The Porvoo Common Statement* says: 'The bishop gathers together those who are ordained to share in the tasks of ministry and to represent the concerns of the community' (*Together in Mission and Ministry: The Porvoo Common Statement,* para. 44, p. 25).

Thus the bishop who is a member of the universal episcopal college is also a member of the ministerial team in a particular diocese, and its leader. In this way the personal ministry of oversight is supported by those with whom the bishop shares in ordained ministry. Some use the term 'collegiality' to describe this wider sharing of ministry. However, this broader use of the term may obscure the particular quality of shared episcopal ministry with its formal structures.

Bishops meet together collegially in each of the provinces of the Anglican Communion, while the Lambeth Conference expresses the collegiality of bishops in a concrete way at the international level. Though the Conference is not a legislative body, it offers a unique experience to bishops who come from churches with different cultures and social and political contexts, and with different agendas and problems, to live and worship together in fellowship and to learn from each other. The Conference provides an opportunity every ten years to address issues which touch the unity and mission of the Church. Although they have no juridical authority, the Resolutions of the Lambeth Conference carry a considerable moral authority by virtue of the office of oversight entrusted to those who gather to take counsel. Their decisions need to be received with attentiveness and put to a process of discernment and reception.

In the Anglican Communion, the collegiality of bishops is always understood within the conciliarity of the whole body. Hence the language of bishop in synod is a characteristic expression of Anglican polity. From the conciliar movement the churches of the Reformation learned the necessity of involving non-episcopal clergy and representative laity in the governance of the Church. Nevertheless, in matters of doctrine and worship bishops have a special responsibility, though even in these matters their guidance is always put to the discernment and reception of the people of God. The presence of the elected non-episcopal members of the Anglican Consultative Council (presbyters, and lay men and women) is a reminder of the conciliar life of the Church to which the collegial ministry of bishops belongs.

4

The Ministry of Oversight: Issues of Power and Authority

Both as a divinely ordained community and as a human institution, the Christian Church is necessarily involved in the exercise of power and authority. Great care is required to ensure that these are experienced as beneficial and salutary. The power of God is at work in the Church through the Holy Spirit (Romans 15.13) and the authority of God is mediated through the Church by virtue of its apostolic mission (Matthew 28. 18-20). The reality of the distribution and exercise of power and authority in the Church needs to be acknowledged in any attempt to understand the collegial ministry of oversight and its place and role within the conciliar life of the Church. The report of the Anglican – Roman Catholic International Commission, *The Gift of Authority*, points out that, though 'the exercise of authority can be oppressive and destructive', 'authority rightly exercised is a gift of God to bring reconciliation and peace to humankind' (para. 5).

Power and authority are notoriously difficult to define and to distinguish in a way that commands broad assent. For our purposes, earthly power may be provisionally defined as the ability of a person or group to achieve effects on others, individually or collectively, intentionally or not; and authority may be defined as the recognition, legitimation or acceptance of that power by those who are so affected. This way of defining and distinguishing the two concepts is not far removed from the New Testament's own usage. There all power and all authority to use it are seen to derive ultimately from God, though they may be perverted by human sin and superhuman evil.

The Greek New Testament speaks of both power (*dynamis*) and authority (*exousia*). These terms are sometimes distinguished and sometimes used synonymously, or virtually so. Whatever nuances may be discerned in the

Greek, power and authority are bound up together. The Gospels and Epistles acknowledge the reality of the sheer power or spiritual strength evidenced in the healing and delivering ministries of Jesus and Paul. *Dynamis* is primarily a phenomenon and does not inherently imply a favourable value judgement – sometimes quite the reverse (Luke 10.19; Acts 3.12; 1 Corinthians 15.24; 2 Thessalonians 2.9; Revelation 13.2) – though it may sometimes do so (Matthew 11.21; Mark 9.1). *Dynamis* is not normally self-validating but needs to be justified. The New Testament writings tend, therefore, to be more concerned with the God-given and God-accountable right to exercise such power, that is to say, with the *authority* evinced by Jesus Christ and subsequently by St Paul. *Exousia* generally (though not always: cf. 1 Corinthians 15.24) refers to the moral right to use power (Mark 2.10; Matthew 28.18). The New Testament affirms that God has given authority to Jesus and to Paul for the sake of salvation, to build up and not to break down. This is borne out by the root meaning of our English word 'authority' which derives from the Latin *auctoritas*: the ability to make increase, to cause to grow, to strengthen or enlarge. Thus an *auctor* (from which derives the English 'author') is a doer, causer, creator, founder, or leader. Authority is intended for the sake of life and growth.

In the light of the endemic post-modern suspicion of all manifestations of power and authority, we need to insist that power and authority are inescapable facets of all forms of community. Power enables things to happen and makes change and development possible, but it can be put to helpful or harmful uses. Power can be intimidating. It can be abused and used for self-aggrandisement. In its more insidious forms, as psychological manipulation, it can induce people to act against their own best interests. In modern social theory, the power wielded by political and religious leaders has been subjected to searching psychological and sociological analysis. In our culture generally, both power and authority tend to be regarded with suspicion. The legitimation of power, as authority, is frequently seen as a social construction intended to serve the interests of those who enjoy political or economic prestige and privilege.

The words and actions of bishops have the power to affect the lives of many people, especially devout church people, and are experienced as either affirming or undermining, building confidence or destroying it.

Groups and individuals who feel marginal to the mainstream of church life are particularly vulnerable. Clergy and laity with a fragile sense of self-esteem set great store by the signals they believe they receive from their bishop, for good or ill. Because they are guardians, providers, leaders and mentors, the bishops, collectively as a House or college and individually in their dioceses, are the recipients of projections that cast them in the role of good or bad authority figures and in either case raise unrealistic expectations.

The exercise of power in the Church should be tempered and chastened by accountability to God. It should be shaped and moulded into conformity to Christ's death and resurrection. The power of the crucified Lord is the only power that properly belongs to his body. It is a vulnerable power that refuses the sword and the legions of angels (Matthew 26.52). It is a self-sacrificing power (John 10.18) and one that reverses the order of the world, putting down the mighty from their seats and raising up the humble (Luke 1.52). The power of God – and therefore every form of power in the Church – takes the way of the cross and lives under the sign of the cross.

Even from the beginning, the Church found that teaching hard to understand and difficult to follow. At the Last Supper a dispute began as to which of the disciples should be considered the greatest (Luke 22.24). In reply, Jesus pointed to his own example: 'I am among you as one who serves' (Luke 22.27). His leadership and authority and that of the apostles remains, but new ideals are established for it. In a highly paradoxical way, the normally antithetical roles of leader and servant are joined together. *Diakonia* in the New Testament is service that has authority, divinely commissioned ministry. The Lord's washing of the disciples' feet, given as an example to them (John 13.2-7), challenges church leaders in every age to interrogate their use of power against that of Jesus Christ. Throughout history the love of money, social status and domination have infected the exercise of leadership in the Church. In *Ut Unum Sint* the Pope acknowledges the existence of sinful structures as one of the causes of division in the Church (para. 34). Any exercise of authority in the Church must be informed both by an understanding of the nature and being of God as revealed in Christ crucified and risen, and also by an acknowledgement of the fact that Christ's authority is mediated particularly through those who themselves are subject to the limitations and sinfulness of human nature.

Pastoral discipline is a proper and necessary use of authority in the Church. It is primarily the responsibility of bishops. They exercise this responsibility in the context of canon law which belongs to the ordering of all churches. In Anglicanism canon law is made through representative, synodical forms of church government and thus can be said to have the consent of the governed (the Anglican faithful). The jurisdiction of bishops carries the responsibility to apply and, where necessary, to enforce canon law. While the diocesan bishop is the chief pastor of all within his diocese and has jurisdiction 'except in places and over persons exempt by law or custom' (Canon C18), in a pluralist society, pastoral oversight of the laity is largely voluntarily accepted and cannot be enforced except where the ordinances of the Church (e.g. regarding marriage) are concerned. Lay officers and lay ministers, such as churchwardens and readers, however, stand in a special relationship to the oversight of the diocesan bishop. Clergy, on the other hand, commit themselves to accept the pastoral oversight of their bishop, and to conduct their lives and ministries under the laws of the Church of England, by the terms of their ordination and licensing. Deacons and presbyters promise to obey their Ordinary 'in all things lawful and honest', while bishops, who are also under the canon law of the Church, are subject to the metropolitical authority of the archbishop. Where canonical discipline has to be enforced, the bishop will seek appropriate advice and assistance and the right of appeal to the archbishop of the province remains. Always discipline should be tempered with pastoral concern. 'He is to be merciful, but with firmness, and to minister discipline, but with mercy' (*ASB* Ordination of a Bishop).

In today's society all forms of power and authority are under scrutiny and have to win recognition and acceptance. We are aware of the danger of creating dependence through the exercise of authority. Criticism and challenge are healthy, but 'debunking' and cynicism are corrosive of communal values. On the other hand, authority needs to be accountable to the community in order to be acceptable. Ultimate accountability is to God whose authority is mediated through the Church. But there is also a mutual accountability of those entrusted with oversight, in the interests of fairness and consistency.

There is a proper accountability between pastor and faithful focused in representative conciliar channels. In the Church of England, lay and clerical synod representatives are elected by their respective constituencies. Lay and clerical voices play their part in the complex system of appointment and election of diocesan bishops. (Other churches of the Anglican Communion elect their bishops as well.) Representatives should not merely speak for particular interest groups but should give a voice to the voiceless.

Through the responsible use of representative conciliar channels the mind of the whole people of God can be built up. 'The perception of God's will for the Church does not only belong to the ordained ministry but is shared by all its members' (ARCIC, *Final Report, Authority I*, para. 6).

Within the *koinonia* of the Church, the living experience of communion with God and Christian brothers and sisters in the Spirit, the right exercise of authority is subject to the *sensus fidei* – the gift of spiritual perception and discernment, the God-given sense of what is of God – that comes through the Spirit indwelling the body of Christ and is nurtured through prayer, Bible study and worship. This indwelling enables believers to recognize the voice of the Good Shepherd speaking through their pastors. This process of reception gives rise to the prevailing settled conviction (*consensus fidelium*) of the truth – or otherwise – of doctrine, morals and policy, the Scriptures being the touchstone of truth.

5

Collegiality Today in the Service of *Koinonia*

Summary

Chapter 1 explored the Church as *koinonia* as the appropriate context for understanding the conciliar and collegial life of the Church. Chapter 2 looked at the bonds of communion, the gifts of grace, that help to maintain the Church's fidelity to its Lord and equip it for effective mission in the world. Chapter 3 explored the theme of collegiality in the context of collegiality and primacy. Chapter 4 looked at issues of power and authority in relation to the ministry of oversight.

Within the total life of the Church, collegiality is exercised by bishops as representative ministers. Collegiality is an expression of the working together of the people of God and also a means of keeping them together. The collegial ministry of bishops belongs within a connectedness of gracious belonging, operating at the local, national and international spheres of the life of the Church. These levels of the Church's life are not independent but inter-dependent.

Episcopal collegiality exists to ensure the Church's fidelity to the apostolic teaching and mission and to maintain the local church/diocese in fellowship – in communion – with the Church around the world today and the Church throughout the ages. It is a ministry which seeks to hold God's gift of himself in the present in continuity with the memory of the past and the anticipation of the future. It is a ministry with a particular care for continuity and unity.

Because of the divisions of the churches, collegiality today necessarily includes a special concern for maintaining relations with other traditions and ecclesial bodies, especially when matters of faith, order and moral life threaten the Church's unity and communion.

The bishops as a college have a special responsibility to nurture the unity and continuity of the Church. They also have a special responsibility for leading the Church in response to the complex issues of the contemporary world. This entails attentive listening to the challenges which come from new scientific knowledge and new moral dilemmas, as well as the questions posed to the Christian faith by other faith communities and new movements of spirituality. Collegiality entails listening to those on the margins of the Church, the prophetic voices, as well as to those outside the Church, in order to discern what should be the authentic witness to the gospel in today's world.

Episcopal collegiality involves leadership in the discernment of truth, bringing into focus matters of concern, and determining what level of the Church's life is the appropriate one for exploring them. It entails determining what needs to be said at any particular moment and after that continuing to show care for the response and reception in the ongoing life of the Church.

The exercise of collegiality requires that each bishop exhibit something of the following qualities:

- faithful discipleship to Jesus Christ grounded in a life of prayer;

- a readiness to listen to the Church and the world;

- sound learning which springs from the study of Scripture, the tradition of the Church and contemporary theological research;

- a willingness to engage with new knowledge in various fields;

- an ability to weigh matters with wisdom;

- a recognition that the mystery of God is always seen 'as in a glass darkly';

- a patience to continue with difficult and seemingly intractable questions;

- a creative imagination to discern the signs of God's kingdom;

- a willingness to make room for different positions when matters are complex and answers as yet unclear;

- a humility to confess mistakes;

- the skill to communicate wisely;

- the courage to take the lead, even when it makes one unpopular;

- the readiness always to be attentive to the prompting of the guidance of the Holy Spirit;

- the willingness and ability to work in partnership with others.

COLLEGIALITY IN THE CHURCH OF ENGLAND

The Church of England is part of the one, holy, catholic and apostolic Church (Canon C15: Preface to the Declaration of Assent). Through the ministry of pastoral oversight (*episkope*) all its people are cared for and brought to participate more fully in the life and mission of the one true God, Father, Son and Holy Spirit. Through its conciliar structures, the whole priestly body of the Church takes responsibility for the provision of the ministry of pastoral oversight and provides the resources for it. However, this ministry of pastoral oversight is exercised at various structural levels: through the bishop, together with his presbyters, in the local church/diocese; through the episcopate meeting collegially in the House of Bishops and bishops' conferences; and through the primacy of the Archbishops of Canterbury and York.

In the Church of England bishops meet collegially with 'those who are ordained to share in the tasks of ministry and to represent the concerns of the community' (*Together in Mission and Ministry: The Porvoo Common Statement*, para. 44, p. 25). The diocesan bishop works collegially with suffragan and assistant bishops and with all fellow presbyters within the diocese. All of them minister 'not in their own names, but in Christ's; and do minister by his commission and authority' (Article XXVI of the Articles of Religion). Together they seek to serve all within the diocese, whether or not people show any religious affiliation.

The House of Bishops

Diocesan bishops, each of whom has jurisdiction within his own diocese, meet together collegially in the House of Bishops. However, a number of suffragan bishops are also members of the House – elected by their fellow suffragans in the two provinces. There is some ambiguity about the representative position which the elected suffragans carry in the House. If all bishops by virtue of consecration share a ministry of collegiality, then there may be an argument for all bishops being members of the House of Bishops. On the other hand, the existence of the Bishops' Meeting and the more recent emergence of regional meetings of bishops may be the more appropriate way of expressing and exercising a wider collegiality. The collegiality of the House of Bishops would then be restricted to those who hold jurisdiction in a diocese. Even then there would remain a degree of anomaly concerning area bishops, who exercise a measure of delegated jurisdiction but who would not be members of the House of Bishops. It is not easy to see how the system could become wholly free from anomaly, without the House itself becoming so large as to render it ineffective. The present arrangement, though open to question, may continue to commend itself in practice as a way of heeding the experience and concerns of suffragans and of making good use of their expertise in various areas. Meanwhile, it is worth noting that, following the General Synod debate on the report *Episcopal Ministry*, the House itself requested that further work should be done on the ministry of suffragan bishops.

Regional meetings of bishops in England

A recent development is for bishops to meet with fellow bishops in regional gatherings. These supplement the formal provincial collegiality of bishops in the Upper Houses of the Convocations. Regional gatherings are neither national nor diocesan. They include all the bishops, diocesan and suffragan, and sometimes leaders with oversight in other churches, in the given region. These meetings exercise no formal authority but nevertheless are valuable for mutual support, for the sharing of local concerns, for common prayer, for strengthening episcopal fellowship. They are increasingly important for reflecting in smaller groups, in greater detail, on complex issues which confront the House of Bishops at the national level. Further, through the close relationships fostered within regional groups, some have been helped to live in the 'highest degree of communion possible', while different opinions are held with integrity on an issue which touches the communion of the Church, such as the issue of the ordination of women (cf. *Eames Commission*). The fellowship provided by these regional meetings of bishops is being recognized as increasingly important for the life of the Church, not least for providing the context for clarifying pressing issues and for maintaining the space necessary for the Church to seek patiently the mind of Christ.

Local, national and regional gatherings of bishops are interrelated and form part of an interlocking experience of the ministry of collegiality. There is a special obligation, for those who are entrusted with oversight, to maintain openness to the wider collegiality of the Church, especially within the Anglican Communion.

Collegial responsibility

Episcopal collegiality is intended to minister within the world and not above it, for its mending and not apart from its suffering. The college must strive to help the people of God become a sign of that recovered and renewed community God calls the Church to be for God's own sake and for the sake of the world – to share the abundant, healing life of God with all, and especially with the broken, the outcast and the needy.

In certain circumstances, not just the representative voice of a bishop, but the united voice of the episcopal college, or of bishops with presbyters and representative lay people, is more telling than an isolated voice. For example, the pastoral care reflected in collegial statements that call for the right treatment of asylum seekers or for the reordering of Third World debt is central to the Church's vital engagement with issues of peace and justice.

Collegiality, discernment and reception

More and more the Church of England looks today for guidance from the House of Bishops on complex issues of faith, order and moral teaching. The discerning of the mind of Christ for the Church is a lengthy and complex process in which bishops, both as individuals and collegially, have a crucial role to play. Their task is to ensure that different voices are heard and that the normative witness of Scripture and the testimony of the Church through the ages is brought to bear on contemporary challenges.

The House of Bishops' statement, *The Nature of Christian Belief* (1986), emphasized 'the function of bishops to listen to the whole people of God, to keep various groups and points of view open to one another, and to promote and guide the sharing of different faith-perceptions in honesty and charity' (para. 65). The bishops can help the Church by ensuring that the work of professional scholars is enlisted. The Church needs the wider resources of different disciplines, and the rigour and criticism of the academic world (para. 69).

It is appropriate that, in the process of discernment, the bishops should make clear the range of views held within the college at any one time. It is not a sign of weakness that, in the process of discernment, different – even opposing – views are held. The role of the bishops is to keep the discussion open until the consensus is formed. Consensus does not necessarily mean coming to a single opinion. It may mean agreeing that for the foreseeable future different views may continue to be held with integrity until the mind of Christ becomes clear, not only for the Church of England, or indeed even the Anglican Communion, but for the whole Church. It is the duty of individual bishops and the college to oversee the ongoing process of discernment and open reception, and to see that those of different opinions go on in dialogue listening to, and learning from, one another.

One sharp question is how far it is legitimate, once the college has come to a common mind, for any individual bishop to teach what is contrary to the consensus of the college. While the Church must make room for the prophetic voice, there is a particular responsibility on bishops to honour the consensus of the college, especially when this has been articulated after careful and prayerful reflection and in consultation with the people of God. Collegiality can sometimes impose limitations on the ministry of a bishop, yet there may be occasions when, in conscience, an individual bishop feels compelled to resist the common mind.

Discerning the mind of Christ for the Church, particularly in the interpretation of doctrine and the provision of forms of worship, is a particular responsibility of the episcopate within the conciliar life of the Church. The

House of Bishops (which, historically, consists of the Upper Houses of the Convocations of Canterbury and York) is part of the synodical structure of the Church of England – though its ministry is certainly not confined to synodical processes. At diocesan level the bishop consults and reflects with fellow clergy and with elected lay people through the diocesan synod and the Bishops' Council. At national level bishops, as a college, consult with clergy and laity through the General Synod. As those entrusted with oversight, the bishops always have the possibility of calling a halt when a matter appears to be going in a direction contrary to the understanding of the college. The faithful have a duty, when called upon, to act with restraint and respect when responding to the lead given by those called and consecrated to do so. The bishops may take a matter to themselves for further reflection and subsequently bring the matter back in such a way that they offer guidance to the Church.

It is vital that all those involved in these processes of discernment and reception understand the need for them and the different roles of bishop, clergy and lay people within them. It is also important that the bishops are alert to the views of other churches and to what those outside the formal structures of the Church have to offer.

Resourcing collegiality

As the Church of England comes to understand the crucial importance of collegiality in serving the Church's communion in faith, life and witness, so it becomes clear that the ministry of collegiality will continue to require adequate and professional resourcing. The boards and councils of the General Synod provide an important resource, both for the Synod itself (and the House of Bishops within it), and also for the bishops in their individual responsibilities in the diocese and the nation. The adequate resourcing of the House – in theological as in other respects – should be kept under regular review, especially as the Church expects more and more of the House and its members.

Collegiality and the Archbishops' Council

Recently the Church of England has been going through a process of change. The Archbishops' Council now plays a central role in its life. It is not yet quite clear what the precise relation of the Council will be to the House of Bishops. We believe that the Archbishops' Council should support the work of the House of Bishops, since the episcopate is called to guard the faith and guide the Church. Each body – the General Synod, the House of Bishops within it and the Archbishops' Council – needs to have a clear understanding of its role within the interlocking structures that make up the web of belonging, and an estimate of its ecclesial significance.

Collegiality and primacy

In the Church of England the Archbishops of Canterbury and York chair meetings of the House of Bishops and its Standing Committee and are chairman and vice-chairman respectively of the Archbishops' Council. They have a particular ministry in drawing out the mind of the college, extending pastoral care and support to the bishops and acting as spokesmen for the college – presenting the mind of the episcopate.

The Archbishops preside in the General Synod, addressing the Synod on matters of current concern in church and world, and from time to time make presidential statements. By virtue of their office as presidents they may intervene in any debate.

COLLEGIALITY IN THE ANGLICAN COMMUNION

The collegiality of bishops ministers to the unity and communion of the Church. Episcopal collegiality is exercised at diocesan, provincial/national, international and global levels. There is a move currently for collegiality to be expressed at regional levels. The bishops of England, Wales, Ireland and Scotland, for example, meet every other year. Within the Anglican Communion there is an international expression of the principle of episcopal collegiality in both the Lambeth Conference and the Primates' Meeting.

The Lambeth Conference

Since 1867, the Lambeth Conference has played a significant role in shaping Anglican identity and maintaining the unity of the Communion. When bishops come together in the Lambeth Conference they come representing their dioceses, the portion of the people of God entrusted to their pastoral care. But they also represent the Communion to their diocese. They thus represent the part to the whole and the whole to the part. A number of questions concerning collegiality at the level of the world Communion are emerging:

1. **In what sense is the Lambeth Conference in fact an expression of episcopal collegiality?** Collegiality belongs to that body of bishops, acting together, whether in a diocese, a province/national church or the universal Church, that has oversight of the Church. Collegiality implies a care for the unity of the Church in faith, sacraments and Christian discipleship. It entails a bearing of one another's burdens, mutual accountability, and a share in the care of all the churches. In all of these ways collegiality supports and does not detract from the responsibility of each bishop in the diocese. The bishops of the Anglican Communion, gathered at the Lambeth Conference, have moral authority to teach and guide the Communion. The Lambeth Conference does not have juridical, binding authority and is certainly not a governing body for the Anglican Communion, which is made up of legally autonomous churches. It is, however, a collegial body because it brings together bishops of the Anglican Communion as representative ministers. On the other hand, the Lambeth Conference is not fully *conciliar*, since it is not a council or synod of the Church. Unlike a council or a synod it does not have a legislative function. And unlike councils and synods as received in the Anglican tradition, elected presbyters and lay people do not participate as members (though all members, presbyteral and lay, of the Anglican Consultative Council are present at a Lambeth Conference).

2.   **What is the relation of the collegiality of the Lambeth Conference to the collegiality of the universal college of bishops?** The bishops of the Anglican Communion meet together to take counsel about matters which affect the unity of the universal Church, including the common faith, the ordering of the Church's life and its ministry, and Christian discipleship in the modern world. That they come from every continent brings a worldwide perspective to the horizons of each. Each is able to contribute local experience to enrich the reflections of the whole. The present divisions of the Church divide the episcopate of the universal Church and impose a limitation on collegiality. Nevertheless, the Lambeth Conference is an authentic and necessary expression of episcopal collegiality at the world level.

3.   **What authority has the Lambeth Conference?** As we have noted, the Lambeth Conference does not have legally binding authority and is not a governing body for the Anglican Communion. Nevertheless, by virtue of the fact that those gathered together have been entrusted with a ministry of oversight, its resolutions have considerable moral authority and are offered for reception by the member churches. Although the member churches are legally autonomous, they are actually interdependent. Interdependence requires the support of appropriate structures and adequate resources.

Greater structural interdependence would require a clear resolution of the relationship between the Anglican Consultative Council as presently constituted and the Lambeth Conference itself. At present the Anglican Consultative Council consists of elected laity, presbyters and deacons, as well as bishops, and thus clearly has some characteristics of a representative conciliar body. However, like the Lambeth Conference, the ACC lacks legislative authority and is therefore not fully conciliar. Moreover, its bishops, clergy and laity do not constitute 'houses' which can sit separately, if required. Moreover, as currently constituted its relationship to the Lambeth Conference is unclear. Its lay and clerical members attend the Lambeth Conference, though not as voting members. Resolution III.6(d) of the 1998 Lambeth Conference recommended that the bishops who represent each province of the communion on the ACC should be the primates of the provinces.

The Virginia Report has asked whether Anglicans can continue as a world communion with merely morally authoritative but not juridically binding decision-making structures at the international level. Since 1867, the Lambeth Conferences have consistently resisted suggestions that they should claim or seek juridical powers and an authority binding on the member churches. In his opening address to the first Lambeth Conference Archbishop Longley stated:

> It has never been contemplated that we should assume the functions of a general synod of all the churches in full communion with the Church of England, and take upon ourselves to enact canons that should be binding upon those represented. (*The Six Lambeth Conferences*, p. 8)

The Conference of 1948 observed: 'Former Lambeth Conferences have . . . rejected proposals for a formal primacy of Canterbury, for an Appellate Tribunal, and for giving the Conference the status of a legislative synod. The Lambeth Conference remains advisory' (*Lambeth Conference 1948*, pt. 2, p. 84).

The wider fellowship of episcopally ordered churches

A welcome enrichment of the Lambeth Conference is provided by the participation of other bishops in communion with the Archbishop of Canterbury. All the bishops of the churches of South Asia, where Anglicans have united with Christians of other traditions, were present for the first time in 1998 as full participant members with a right both to speak and to vote. There were also representative bishops of other churches in communion: the Old Catholic churches of the Union of Utrecht, the Mar Thoma Church, the Philippine Independent Church and the Nordic and Baltic churches of the Porvoo Communion. These bishops played an active part, while not voting. In addition to bishops of churches in communion, the ecumenical participants (formerly observers) brought the experience of the wider Christian community to the Conference. This expressed a fuller collegiality in the service of the unity of Christ's church.

If the Lambeth Conference is to acquire a stronger collegial character, there will be a need for fuller consultation and greater mutual account- ability. However, it will be important at the same time to safeguard the liberty for appropriate diversity which is such a valued part of the Anglican way.

The Primates' Meeting

Collegiality benefits from a ministry of primacy to preside within the collegial and conciliar life of the Church. There is a special role for the primates who are seen as 'brothers among brothers' in their provinces. At the world level Anglicans have increasingly experienced the special role of the Archbishop of Canterbury within the Communion as a whole. Full consideration of primacy at the provincial/national and international levels is beyond the scope of this paper. Further work is needed on this subject and was called for by the 1998 Lambeth Conference (Resolution III.8(h)), which set primacy firmly in the context of episcopal collegiality. The 1998 Lambeth Conference recommended an enhanced collegial voice for the Primates' Meeting, under the presidency of the Archbishop of Canterbury, 'in offering guidance on doctrinal, moral and pastoral matters' and asked that it should give positive encouragement in mission (Resolution III.6(a)(b)).

COLLEGIALITY IN AN ECUMENICAL AGE

Anglicans maintain that their ministry is the ministry of the one, holy, catholic and apostolic Church – the universal Church. A bishop is a bishop of the universal Church and belongs to the universal episcopal college. Because of the divisions of the churches there is *de facto* no universal collegial exercise of oversight. However, the ecumenical movement of the twentieth century has increasingly made possible a degree of shared over- sight. This is true for Anglicans at the diocesan, national and worldwide levels. Further development of shared oversight is being explored in a number of ecumenical conversations.

At the diocesan level, almost every diocese has some structure in place for bishops to share together in oversight and leadership with those who have been entrusted with *episkope* in other churches. In many places church leaders sign formal covenants which commit them to share together in witness. In Liverpool Archbishop Derek Worlock, Bishop David Sheppard and latterly the Revd Dr John Newton showed what is possible in the sharing of oversight. Where local churches share together, especially in formally constituted Local Ecumenical Partnerships, Christians begin to look for a shared leadership which mirrors their local experience. Shared oversight is also focused in the office of the Ecumenical Moderator of Milton Keynes. Many of the diocesan responses to *Called To Be One* pleaded for a more prophetic ministry of shared oversight. As a result of the Porvoo Agreement English diocesan bishops are beginning to share oversight with their Nordic colleagues for Lutheran congregations in their dioceses. A similar arrangement is emerging in some of the Nordic countries for the chaplaincies of the Church of England Diocese in Europe.

However, there are obstacles in the way. The difference in the boundaries of the areas over which the church leaders exercise oversight, the difference in size of church membership and the different structures of authority and patterns of pastoral care often make sharing leadership time-consuming and frustrating. In spite of this, there are opportunities to experience different patterns and models of oversight and to compare the different ethos and expectations attached to the ministry of oversight in the different traditions. In places Anglicans have an opportunity to see women exercising a ministry of oversight.

At the national (and European) level collegial gatherings work almost in complete isolation, although even here there are signs that progress is being made. One result of the Meissen, Porvoo and Fetter Lane Agreements is that representative bishops from time to time attend meetings of the House of Bishops. The Porvoo churches have a regular meeting of church leaders (episcopal, presbyteral and lay) and their primates also meet from time to time.

Periodically the House of Bishops of the Church of England and the Chairmen of Districts of the Methodist Church meet to consider matters of common concern. The Archbishops of Canterbury and York meet each year with leaders of the Methodist Church in England.

There are, however, many occasions at the national level when a greater degree of shared oversight could serve the unity and mission of the Church in this country. The joint statement of the Roman Catholic Bishops of England and Wales and the House of Bishops of the Church of England on euthanasia was a good example of what could be achieved. Many Anglicans welcomed the statement of the Roman Catholic Bishops, *The Common Good,* and only wished that it could have been a joint statement. Similarly, the earlier report *Faith in the City* might have had even greater impact had it been a joint venture. There are many opportunities in this country for joint Christian witness in social, political and economic issues. It is easier to do it alone but is more effective and credible to think and act together. Joint efforts build *koinonia* and increase the desire for greater visible unity, in which there would be a single episcopal collegial ministry in the service of the mission of the one Church.

Summary and Conclusion

Conciliarity, collegiality and primacy in the service of *koinonia*

Koinonia is the life of the people of God, a participation in 'the grace of the Lord Jesus Christ, the love of God and the communion (*koinonia*) of the Holy Spirit' (2 Corinthians 13.13). The Holy Spirit draws us into fellowship (*koinonia*) with the Father and the Son and opens the way for us to have fellowship with one another (1 John 1.3-7). *Koinonia* is the quality of corporate life enjoyed in the Church in which the fullness of Christ is present. The whole body of the faithful, partaking of the means of grace – principally word, sacrament and pastoral care – is united to its Head and attains more and more to the full stature of Christ (Ephesians 4.13).

The ministry of Christ in his body is channelled through every member, graced with gifts of the Spirit (1 Corinthians 12.4-12). For all who have passed from darkness to light through baptism, with its Trinitarian confession of faith, are incorporated into Christ's messianic, Spirit-bearing body (1 Corinthians 12.13) and are anointed as a prophetic, royal priesthood (1 Peter 2.5-9). Within this universal royal priesthood of the baptized there is a divine economy at work: special representative ministries are given authority and grace to speak and act in a public way on behalf of Christ and the Church, as they preach and teach the word, celebrate the sacraments and provide pastoral oversight.

Koinonia is expressed in conciliarity, the whole Church taking responsibility for its life by coming together to take counsel in a representative and constitutional way for its wellbeing and the most effective serving of God's mission in the world. Conciliarity requires both the personal and collegial exercise of oversight in order to strengthen coherence and cohesion in the Church. Collegiality, in its turn, can be enhanced by a ministry of primacy, to preside within the conciliar and collegial life of the Church. The personal, collegial and communal (conciliar) aspects of the exercise of authority in leadership, consultation and decision-making belong together, providing mutual support and mutual criticism. Thus the Church is equipped to praise and glorify God through Jesus Christ in the power of the Holy Spirit and to serve the gracious purposes of God's coming kingdom.

52

References

ASB: The Alternative Service Book 1980

ARCIC, *Church as Communion*, Church House Publishing and CTS, 1991.

ARCIC, *The Final Report of the Anglican – Roman Catholic International Commission*, SPCK/CTS, 1982.

ARCIC, *The Gift of Authority* (Authority in the Church III), CTS, Anglican Book Centre, Church Publishing Incorporated, July 1999.

BEM: Baptism, Eucharist and Ministry, WCC, 1982.

Called To Be One, Churches Together in England, 1996.

The Common Good and the Catholic Church's Social Teaching, St Gabriel's Communications, 1996.

Dogmatic Constitution on the Church (Lumen Gentium) (W. M. Abbot, ed.), *The Documents of Vatican II*, Geoffrey Chapman, 1965.

The Eames Commission: The Official Reports: The Archbishop of Canterbury's Commission on Women in the Episcopate, Anglican Book Centre, Toronto, 1994.

Episcopal Ministry: The Report of the Archbishops' Group on the Episcopate 1990, Church House Publishing, 1990.

Eucharistic Presidency: A Theological Statement by the House of Bishops of the General Synod, Church House Publishing, 1997.

Faith in the City: A Call for Action by Church and Nation: The Report of the Archbishop of Canterbury's Commission on Urban Priority Areas, Church House Publishing, 1985.

GROU: God's Reign and Our Unity: The Report of the Anglican – Reformed International Commission, SPCK/St Andrew Press, 1984.

Issues in Human Sexuality: A Statement by the House of Bishops, Church House Publishing, 1991.

The Lambeth Conference 1948: Encyclical Letter from the Bishops together with the Resolutions and Reports, SPCK, 1948.

May They All Be One: A Response of the House of Bishops of the Church of England to Ut Unum Sint, Church House Publishing, 1997.

The Nature of Christian Belief: A Statement and Exposition of the House of Bishops of the General Synod of the Church of England, Church House Publishing, 1986.

The Priesthood of the Ordained Ministry, Board for Mission and Unity, 1986.

The Six Lambeth Conferences 1867–1920, SPCK, 1920.

Synodical Government in the Church of England: A Review, Church House Publishing, 1997.

Together in Mission and Ministry: The Porvoo Common Statement with Essays on Church and Ministry in Northern Europe, Church House Publishing, 1993.

Towards a Church of England Response to BEM and ARCIC, CIO Publishing, 1985.

Ut Unum Sint: *Commitment to Ecumenism,* John Paul II, Vatican City, Catholic Truth Society, 1995.

The Virginia Report: The Report of the Inter-Anglican Theological and Doctrinal Commission, ACC, 1997.

Working as One Body: The Report of the Archbishops' Commission on the Organisation of the Church of England, Church House Publishing, 1995.